The Nesting Ground

The Nesting Ground

∿ A BOOK OF POEMS

by David Wagoner

INDIANA UNIVERSITY PRESS
Bloomington

The poems "The Satirists" (1960); and "A Guide to Dungeness Spit," "That Old Gang of Mine," and "A Séance for Two Hands" (1962) were copyrighted in the respective years shown by *The Hudson Review*. "The Emergency Maker," "Offertory," "Once Upon a Picnic Ground," "A Day in the City," "The Nesting Ground" (1962); and "The Breathing Lesson," "Advice to the Orchestra," "On Seeing an X-Ray of My Head" (1963) were copyrighted in the respective years shown by *Poetry*. "Elegy for Simon Corl, Botanist," "In the Fiction Class" (under the title "The Teaching Load") (1959); "The Trophy," "Every Good Boy Does Fine," "No Sale" (1962) were copyrighted in the respective years shown by *Saturday Review*. "The Famine of Reason" and "The First Day of a Search" (1959) were copyrighted by *Poetry Northwest*. "Chrysalis" and "Out for a Night" were published in *The Massachusetts Review* (1962). "Filling Out a Blank" and "Song in the Dead of Summer" were copyrighted in 1962 by *Prairie Schooner*. "The Observer" (under the title "Watching") was published in *The Observer* (London), 1962. "Free Passage" and "Plumage" were published in *Choice*, 1963. "After Consulting My Yellow Pages" (1959), "Homage" (1961), "The Calculation" (1962), and "Closing Time" (1963) were copyrighted in the respective years shown by The New Yorker Magazine, Inc. "Diary" was published in *International Literary Annual No. 2*, edited by John Wain (London: John Calder, Ltd., 1959), copyright by John Calder, Ltd.

To Patt, with love.

Contents

Diary   9
A Guide to Dungeness Spit   10
The Nesting Ground   12
Closing Time   14
After Consulting My Yellow Pages   15
Homage   16
The Emergency Maker   17
Free Passage   19
The Calculation   20
Séance for Two Hands   22
Elegy for Simon Corl, Botanist   23
The Holding Place   24
Offertory   25
In the Fiction Class   26
The Trophy   27
Plumage   28
Once upon a Picnic Ground   29
To the Master of *Sea Bird* of Friday Harbor   30
No Sale   32
Coots Going Away   34
The Skate's Egg   35
The Watch   36
The Breathing Lesson   38
The Famine of Reason   39
Song in the Dead of Summer   40
Chrysalis   41
The Satirists   42
Advice to the Orchestra   43
The Starlings   45
The First Day of a Search   47
Out for a Night   49
On the Dosewallips Bridge   50
Writing to Order   52
That Old Gang of Mine   54
The Carcass   56

A Day in the City   58
Standing Halfway Home   60
On Seeing an X-Ray of My Head   61
Every Good Boy Does Fine   62
Filling Out a Blank   63
The Observer   64

Diary

At Monday dawn, I climbed into my skin
And went to see the money. There were the shills:
I conned them—oh, the coins fell out of their mouths,
And paint peeled from the walls like dollar bills.
Below their money-belts, I did them in.

All day Tuesday, grand in my underwear,
I shopped for the world, bought basements and airplanes,
Bargained for corners and pedestrians
And, when I'd marketed the elms away,
Swiped from the water, stole down to the stones.

Suddenly Wednesday offered me my shirt,
Trousers, and shoes. I put them on to dream
Of the one-way stairway and the skittering cloud,
Of the dangerous, footsore crossing at the heart
Where trees, rivers, and stones reach for the dead.

And the next day meant the encircling overcoat
Wherein I sweltered, woolly as a ram:
From butt to swivel, I hoofed it on the loam,
Exacting tribute from the flock in the grass.
My look passed through the werewolf to the lamb.

Friday shied backwards, pulling off my clothes:
The overcoat fell open like a throat;
Shirt-tail and shoe went spidery as a thought,
And covetous drawers whipped knee-deep in a knot.
My skin in a spiral tapered into gold.

And it was naked Saturday for love
Again: the graft grew milky at a kiss.
I lay on the week with money, lust, and vapor,
Megalomania, fear, the tearing-off,
And love in a coil. On Sunday, I wrote this.

A Guide to Dungeness Spit

Out of wild roses down from the switching road between pools
We step to an arm of land washed from the sea.
On the windward shore
The combers come from the strait, from narrows and shoals
Far below sight. To leeward, floating on trees
In a blue cove, the cormorants
Stretch to a point above us, their wings held out like skysails.
Where shall we walk? First, put your prints to the sea,
Fill them, and pause there:
Seven miles to the lighthouse, curved yellow-and-grey miles
Tossed among kelp, abandoned with bleaching rooftrees,
Past reaches and currents;
And we must go afoot at a time when the tide is heeling.
Those whistling overhead are Canada geese;
Some on the waves are loons,
And more on the sand are pipers. There, Bonaparte's gulls
Settle a single perch. Those are sponges.
Those are the ends of bones.
If we cross to the inner shore, the grebes and goldeneyes
Rear themselves and plunge through the still surface,
Fishing below the dunes
And rising alarmed, higher than waves. Those are cockleshells.
And these are the dead. I said we would come to these.
Stoop to the stones.
Overturn one: the grey-and-white, inch-long crabs come pulsing
And clambering from their hollows, tiptoeing sideways.
They lift their pincers
To defend the dark. Let us step this way. Follow me closely
Past snowy plovers bustling among sand-fleas.
The air grows dense.
You must decide now whether we shall walk for miles and miles
And whether all birds are the young of other creatures
Or their own young ones,
Or simply their old selves because they die. One falls,
And the others touch him webfoot or with claws,

Treading him for the ocean,
This is called sanctuary. Those are feathers and scales.
We both go into mist, and it hooks behind us.
Those are foghorns.
Wait, and the bird on the high root is a snowy owl
Facing the sea. Its flashing yellow eyes
Turn past us and return;
And turning from the calm shore to the breakers, utterly still,
They lead us by the bay and through the shallows,
Buoy us into the wind.
Those are tears. Those are called houses, and those are people.
Here is a stairway past the whites of our eyes.
All our distance
Has ended in the light. We climb to the light in spirals,
And look, between us we have come all the way,
And it never ends
In the ocean, the spit and image of our guided travels.
Those are called ships. We are called lovers.
There lie the mountains.

The Nesting Ground

Piping sharp as a reed,
The small bird stood its ground
Twenty feet from ours.
From the shore, another answered
(The piercing double note
Meant killdeer and killdeer)
And skimmed over the sand,
Over the sparse grass,
Lit, then scurried away,
Flopping, crooking its wing
To flash a jagged streak
And the amber of its back.

When the first bird moved a foot
And struck out at the air,
Two chicks leaped after it,
Their plain heads clear as day.
We walked straight to the spot,
Needing to stir what we love,
Knelt down and found nothing,
Not even when we stared
Each checkered, pebbly stalk
Into its own semblance.
We flattened disbelief
With the four palms of our hands.

But the grown birds broke themselves,
Crippled their cries and wings
So near us, we stood up
To follow their sacrifice
That tempts the nails of creatures
Who, needing flight, forget
Whatever they might have caught
By standing still instead.
We kept on walking, led

By pretended injuries,
Till we were far away,
Then turned, as the birds turned
To sail back to the source
Where we had touched our knees,
And saw through our strongest glass
The young spring out of cover,
Piping one death was over.

Closing Time

At midnight, flaking down like chromium
Inside the tavern, light slips off the bar
And tumbles in our laps. The tumbler falling
Off the edge of the table goes to pieces
As quick as mercury around our shoes.
Goodnight to shuffleboard and counter-check.
The last ball-bearing pins its magnet down
And sinks into a socket like the moon.

Over the rings around our eyes, the clock
Says time to decipher wives, husbands, and cars
On keychains swinging under bleary light.
Goodnight to folding friends on the parking lot
As parallel as windows in a wallet.
Lined up like empties on the curb, goodnight
To all who make the far side of the street,
Their eyelids pressed as tight as bottlecaps.

Goodnight to those with jacks as openers,
Those whose half-cases chill their pelvises,
And those with nothing on tap all day tomorrow
Who wind up sleeping somewhere cold as stars,
Who make the stairs and landings, but not doors,
Those in the tubs, or hung on banisters,
Those with incinerators in their arms,
Whose mouths lie open for another one.

Goodnight to drivers driven by themselves
To curve through light years at the straightaway.
Goodnight to cloverleaf and yellow-streak,
To all those leading sheriff's deputies
Over soft shoulders into power-poles,
The red-in-the-face whose teeth hang down by nerves,
The far-afield, the breakers of new ground
Who cartwheel out of sight, end over end.

After Consulting My Yellow Pages

All went well today in the barbers' college:
The razor handles pointed gracefully outward,
The clippers were singing like locusts. And far away
On the fox farms, the red and silver sun brushed lightly
Tail after tail. Happily, the surveyors
Measured the downhill pasture through a theodolite,
Untroubled by birchtrees. The makers of fraternal regalia
Conceived a new star-burst, and the parakeet
In the green bird hospital was coaxed out of danger.
Business came flying out of the horse-meat market,
And under the skillful world, the conduits groped
Forward, heavy with wires, to branch at the lake.
Fish brokers prodded salmon on the walloping dock.
The manifold continuous forms and the luminous products
Emerged, endlessly shining, while the cooling towers
Poured water over themselves like elephants.
Busily the deft hands of the locksmith and wig-maker
In basement and loft, in the magnifying light,
Turned at their labors. The universal joints,
Hose-couplings, elastic hosiery, shingles and shakes,
The well-beloved escrow companies, the heat-exchangers,
Bead-stringers, makers of disappearing beds,
The air-compressors randy with oxygen—
All sprang, remarkably, out of the swinging doors.

And where were you? What did you do today?

Homage

When broken laughter broke
From the edge of a bough
I turned, and a buzzing went
Bushes and yards away
Like a shot and disappeared,
Then quick came humming back
To hang like a red hook
First of all in the air
Embedded in a blur,
Then instantly nowhere.
I glanced from marsh to creek,
To the arches of my eyes
And found flush in the sun
The striking hummingbird
Whirring and chortling down
Faster than I could follow
Within a foot of my ear
Vanishing there and there
Only to reappear
Forty feet aloft,
Unsteady and permanent,
Transfixed, then gone again
To slant straight at my head
But missing, rocketing by.
A streak of redness left
Behind it like a stroke
Bent me down in half,
Bowing me toward its mate
As drab as a burnt leaf
Perched silent at my elbow.

The Emergency Maker

"Still alive—" the message ran,
Tapped on a broken rail—
"The air is somewhere else, the shaft
Is blacker than the coal.
Lower a light and break the rock
That plugged this bloody hole."
But I, who had tossed the dynamite,
Had better things to do
Than juggle stones from here to there
Or bring the dark to day.
Go shovel yourself and hold your nose:
The diggers have to die.

"We'll starve in a week—" the radio said,
Fading in salty weather—
"We've eaten kelp and canvas shoes,
Played at father and mother,
And now we're run out of things to do
To seaweed and each other."
But I, who had drained their compass oil,
Had better fish to fry
Than those I'd caught in a wet canoe
Or over my father's knee.
Go down to the sea and drink your fill:
The lubbers have to die.

"For God's sake—" said the heliograph
High on the mountaintop—
"We're frozen quick on a narrow ledge:
If you want us down, come up.
The avalanche slopes above our heads
Like a nose over a lip."
But I, who had cut their ropes in half,
Gone tumbling down the scree,

Stuffed the crevasse with edelweiss,
And pointed the wrong way,
Said *Pull up your boots and take the air:*
We climbers have to die.

Free Passage

Come away, my sea-lane baggage,
For a crack at the sky.
Come with me in an armlock over the ocean, my china breakage,
We shall go everywhere in a day, grant liberty, squeak, and
         never die.

From docks to lavender palaces,
Oh what comings and goings, my rattan May basket!
Adored as we fall through tissue-paper, through balconies, fountains,
         and trellises,
We shall be borne up like desserts in cream, stuffed like a brisket,

And spun in the air like platters.
At concerts, we shall arrive in all three aisles at once, be lionized in
         jungles, horsed at the seaside.
Chairmen on tiptoe and the giddy, sidelong doctors
Will toast us and be irrevocably toasted.

I have initialed everything, bought floating flashlights,
Filled my binocular flasks with the hottest chutney.
Bye, Mommy! Bye, Daddy! Bye, Sissy! Bye-bye, Fatso!
I'm salting off on the briny with my candy.

Oh my snifter, my tumble-rick, sweet crank of the stars,
My banjo-bottomed, fretful girl,
Tear off those swatches of silk, your hems and haws, and coil them
         up like streamers—
Get set to toss them over the bounding rail.

Sal volatile! Coral uplift! Oh my pink receiver! Freely I swear
Our tanglefoot Rosicrucian wedding on a gangplank, among the
         hoots and the spouting fireboats,
Above flashbulbs, fish-heads, and the drowning divers,
Will be as immortal as rats.

The Calculation

A man six feet tall stands on a curb, facing a light suspended fifteen feet above the middle of a street thirty feet wide. He begins to walk along the curb at five m.p.h. After he has been walking for ten seconds, at what rate is the length of his shadow increasing?

—a problem given by my calculus instructor,
Penn State, 1946

Facing a streetlight under batty moths
And June bugs ratcheting like broken clock-springs,
I stand, for the sake of a problem, on the curb—
Neither in grass nor gutter—while those wings
Switch down the light and patch my undershirt.

I turn half-right. My shadow cuts a hedge,
Climbs through a rhododendron to a porch,
And nods on a windowsill. How far it goes
I leave to burglars and Pythagoras.
Into the slanting glare I slant my watch,

Then walk five miles per hour, my shoes on edge
In a practiced shuffle past the sewer grid
Over the gold no-parking-or-pausing zones
And into the clear —five seconds— into dirt,
Then over a sawhorse studded with lanterns,

And at the tenth I stiffen like a stump
Whose lopped head ripples with concentric figures,
Note the location of my other head
In a garden, but keep trundling forward,
Ignoring *Doppelgängers* from moon and lawn-lamp,

My eyes alert now, leveling my feet,
Seeing my shadow sweeping like a scythe
Across the stalks of daisies, barking trees,

And scraping up the blistered weatherboard
To the eaves of houses, scaling the rough shingles.

At fifteen seconds, in a vacant lot,
My head lies on a board. I count it off.
I think back to the garden, and I guess,
Instructor, after fifteen years of sweat,
It was increasing five feet plus per second.

At the start, I could have fallen, turned around,
Or crossed to the very center of confusion,
My shadow like a manhole, no one's length,
Or the bulb itself been broken with a shot,
And all my reckoning have gone unreckoned.

But I was late because my shadow was
Pointing toward nothing like the cess of light,
Sir, and bearing your cold hypotenuse—
That cutter of corners, jaywalker of angles—
On top of my head, I walked the rest of the night.

Séance for Two Hands

When all the shades could spell
On slates as though at school
Or rap on the wall,
Life was doing well.
Out of the cracks in marble,
From under the lifted table
Came the shape of the soul:
The wind in a shirt-tail,
A fish in a white veil,
The moon behind an owl.
Though put to bed with a shovel
The body like a wheel
Rose from its rut at will
Nor kept the spirit level.

But the dead no longer press
Against the looking-glass.
They have gone out of the gauze,
Away from the feet of yews;
Their lips no longer pause
At the edges of lilies.
Disenthralled from cats' eyes,
Battered from the cows,
Dropped from the breasts of crows,
Driven from the flies,
The ghosts of the latter days
Of the soul's progress
Needle a point in space.
Death alone haunts our house.

Elegy for Simon Corl, Botanist

With wildflowers bedded in his mind,
My blind great-uncle wrote a book.
His lips and beard were berry-stained,
Wrist broken like a shepherd's crook.

His door leaned open to the flies,
And May, like tendrils, wandered in.
The earth rose gently to his knees;
The clouds moved closer than his skin.

Sun against ear, he heard the slight
Stamen and pistil touch for days,
Felt pollen cast aslant like light
Into the shadows of his eyes.

When autumn stalked the leaves, he curled;
His fingers ripened like the sky;
His ink ran to a single word,
And the straight margin went awry.

When frost lay bristling on the weeds,
He smoothed it with a yellow thumb,
Followed his white cane to the woods
Between the saxifrage and thyme,

And heard the hornets crack like ice,
Felt worms arch backward in the snow;
And while the mites died under moss,
The clean scar sang across his brow.

The Holding Place

Strained in an arch, the salmon on her side
In the shallow river beats against the stones,
Her tail gone ragged, body bent to work
At the nesting hollow, flailing in the stream;
She rights herself, falls sideways, but returns
To the racking stretch where she has held for days.

A male behind her vaults across her wake
And slaps his piebald body into foam,
Heaves her aside to flutter and lose way
Down rips of current; in spasms, they fight back.
Through flank and fin, the white beginnings of bones
Are shining out like broken water now.

And tumbling past them with their mouths agape—
Who once were strong as rapids, whose ripe spawn
Was spilled and fathered, buried in a day—
The dead go downstream swiftly, at their ease,
While gull and crow, blue heron and osprey
Cry down to greet them, lifted to the shore.

Offertory

Ready to leave for work, I look around
To check windows and switches: in the sink,
A pool of coffee poured from the last cup
Gleams near the drain; the ring in the bath
At its own level holds my body up;
And crumpled on the bed, blankets like sheep
Crouch where the ram came, reeling, from his dip.
So many rituals: two cups for the gods
Of the left and right temple, the grounds gone
Where all libations go; on porcelain,
My yesterday in an upright, shrinking lather;
Dial down and ticking under the pillow-slip,
Two sheets to the wind hauled back from sleep—
I leave these for the maker of light whose rain
On the alarming morning fell again.

In the Fiction Class

Girls write stories about little girls
Slumped at pianos or refusing oatmeal;
Passion lies changeable and sweet in their mouths like caramels.

Boys write stories about bums
Dying happily with red faces and black thumbs
In bars or parks where no fathers can write them.

Boys and girls write stories about farmers
And farmers' wives who are interchangeable with horses,
Where always the grasshoppers and weather are growing worse.

Refuse, refuse, say the old girls.
You can't catch bummers majoring in bowels,
The wise boys say. No soap, no cereal, and no scales.

Bums on the cold rocks, yes, girls in hot water—
But let's be rough hired hands and farmers' daughters
Embracing painlessly in the loft at the ends of chapters.

Let's have no reasons and no Ma's or Pa's,
Nothing in mind but comfortable bitter days
When the wind between covers flutters our mortgages.

The Trophy

The size of a thumb and the size of a foot,
Two stories high over the street,
A swallow struck a pigeon straight,
Looped, and sent it down into panic
From pole to roof-ledge, scissoring
Inches and coverts from the tail,
Up and around a wire, and vanished,
While the pigeon staggered to a sill;
But moments later, skimming back,
The swallow in its afterthought
Serenely over the coughing traffic
Sailed a descending figure-eight
With one small feather in its beak,
Dropped it to flutter slowly down,
Banked, caught it casually, and ate it.

Plumage

Beside a bush, the pheasant on one foot
Is standing motionless, green head erect,
Bronze belly feathers washing into grass.
He stares to know me. Staring back, I see
Each wing-bar tasselled like a shock of wheat,
The tail grained edgewise, shoulders flaking white,
His buff flank strewn with black, a scarlet cheek
Cupped to an eye-spot like a flowerhead.

But where? He falls to pieces in my eye—
To flinders, flaws of intersecting light
Where dust and the veins of leaves are cancelled out,
Cross-hatched and baffled at the edge of sight—
And pours all distance forward through a speck
Till stalk and stick, spikelet and ripe seed
Go hedging back as one in the hedgerow.
Too carelessly, I take another breath.

Out of the shadows, booming, rocketing,
Shaking direction, breaking left and right,
The pheasant clappers upward, leaves behind
Nothing in amber, neither claw nor strut,
No gaping side, no parcel of a wing
Clipped off by birdshot as a proof of death.
Flashing across a gulley up the wind,
Again, he drops to pieces in the sun.

Once upon a Picnic Ground

Once upon a picnic ground
Our love was in the bag,
And bread and butter by the pound
Was easily ours to beg.
The nancy boys and gutter girls
Fell over themselves to fetch
The hard-boiled eggs and carrot curls
We needed in the clutch.

And twice upon a picnic ground
Our love lay on the table.
Whenever we passed our plates around,
It gave us heaps of trouble:
Up from our pot of boston beans
Molasses overflowed
And, sticking against our hotdog buns,
Undid the work of God.

When these events were stuffed, we found
Our bag was full of shells,
And ginger bears, without a sound,
Came in their hairy shawls
Through sweet incinerator smoke—
Their muzzles caked with crumbs—
To budge us out of the way and make
A bed for stumblebums.

Now robber jays and pheasant hens
Cry from the hemlock tree
Above the streaming garbagecans
For my lost love and me.
Their craws are full of lightning-bugs;
Their molting feathers cross
On bottles, bags, and bearskin rugs,
And the enduring grass.

To the Master of Sea Bird of Friday Harbor

Wind north-by-east at noon. Sky heavy. The sea light.
Your fishing boat lies portside on the shore.
Through a six-foot hole in the hull
Waves touch and go. Wrack whitens. Eddies go in and out
Among the broken ribs where gravel gathers,
Knocking high as the keel.
If you survived the night, sir, in some luckier boat,
You have lost, in a single blow, motor and rudder,
Binnacle and wheel;
Now held at length by a tangled cable, fragments of mast
Are bobbing away. The chain and anchor
Must have gone down as well.
Here in the hulk, the cabin above my shifting ballast
Has listed ninety degrees to a sleeping quarter;
You have lost the fantail
And bowspirt, most of the starboard strakes, all running lights;
Your sea-blue dungarees lie soaking there
Half under sand
And salted down like fish. The fish caught dead to rights
And held in the hold have broken out of the air
To swim back where you found them
Or to float off as freely as other jetsam. The nets
Have settled down to hold themselves in place.
And if you drowned
In the heaving, heavy slopes, the grey rags of the Strait,
Remember the rules. No passage is endless.
Over rocks, even islands,
The boat came pounding thirty miles to Dungeness Spit
Without your help, throwing away the compass,
Dowsing its lights in the wind,
And tossing its name to pieces. Between the sea and its flights
Against the shore, like fish or men out of water,

Birds on the ground
Will be picked clean for a time. By ancient salvage rights,
I claim this poem from *Sea Bird* of Friday Harbor,
Someday to be returned.

No Sale

Shushing their ankle dogs,
The women behind doors
In curlers, saying No,
All wore their lipstick thin,
Waited till I would go,
Then latched themselves back in.

At the corner in his car
The siding salesman said,
"A high-class canvasser
Tickles them through the screen.
Look them straight in the chest.
Quit telling the truth."

And after pounding weeks
Through showers and heat-waves
At a glance I knew the worst
Weatherboards and shakes
Or paint like blistered heels.
By hundreds of yards and stairs

I talked to all the wives
Who leaned on shaky walls.
I said an engineer
Was waiting at their pleasure
To insulate their sides,
To hold their windows up.

I slummed them, saying floors
Would warp them out of place.
Get ready to play house
Like cards, as serious
As mothers playing trumps.
What else can save your face?

I said a house needs skin
Thicker than powder-base
To stop the sagging, keep
The plaster in its cast,
Packed around bones for years.
But nothing turned their heads.

Swindled by someone else,
They sat in curls all day,
Waiting to be let down,
Waiting to fall straight
And stringy at midnight.
So I went straight, and quit.

Coots Going Away

Slowly, the bunches get up from the lawn
And hobble to the shore, not going in
But squawking in the shallows, looking around
At all the other coots at their wits' end,
Ducking and gawking, each one casting off
Like a scared swimmer paddling for his life,
Neck lunging forward, rear-end up and out,
Each white-billed, red-eyed, sooty-feathered coot
Going away forever, including eggs.
Now on their limp, loose, overgrown green legs
They run across the water, wings like oars,
And beat themselves into the air by force
And skim from sight, needing no shotgun shells
To spur them into falling somewhere else
To settle floating nests in the cattails
Where no men know about the end of rails.

The Skate's Egg

Stopping the car near a boat-ramp to the sea.
"Look, it's a shark's egg." An olive-green case
Ridged with ripe-olive, the size of her own purse,
With hooks like arms and legs at the four corners.
"Sharks don't lay eggs." "Well, something did."
Looking at the chipping scud in the sky.
"Fishermen burn them." Kneeling, touching it:
Springy and fibrous, leathery. "A skate."

Picturing fish like muddy dinner trays.
"Let's open it." Both of us saying so,
Full of a day of cockles and fresh oysters,
Ready to serve and open the whole world.
"Eggs aren't alive until they break themselves."
Getting a wrench from the trunk. The chisel-end.
First, a white ooze stippled with rosy blood.
"Stop." Noticing too late. "It's no use now."

Out of the rip, four milky yolks in a row,
Two whole, two broken, pouring over cinders.
On each, a wildly struggling embryo,
A two-inch, eye-spotted, slender skate in the dirt,
Dying in the sun and wind. Turning away.
Going away from there, shut in our shells.
"We could have hatched them." Nodding yes for no.
"It's simple to keep the ocean in a tub."

The Watch

At the bottom of a box
I found my old self-winding
Graduation watch—
The gift of a good father—
Telling time to be
As much as twice a day
Eleven minutes till three.

I remembered at a glance
Long-, short-, and second-hands
Could stop me in my tracks,
Turn me around, like them
Self-winding on the spot,
And send me running home.

Strapped to my wrist, it sat
For five years, off and on,
Taking and talking back
To my erratic pulse
In a conductor's voice
Whose purpose was to cut
Precisely across noise.

And then I left it off.
Water- and dust-proof,
As blankly luminous,
As safe as it ever was
Against untimely shocks
And the raw, magnetic earth,
It lies in a scrap box.

I watch a bare wrist now,
Not for the works of day
Whose notches turn the years
Out of a creaking shell,
But search in vein and sinew
For what there is to know—
And time enough to tell.

The Breathing Lesson

"Sensations of smell are relatively homogeneous and untranslatable into the form of language. Nobody can enlarge upon an odor."

—Oscar W. Firkins

Around the compass, soap-flakes and burnt corn,
A swamp, the acid cracked from boiling oil,
Sulfur dioxide, plumage of soft coal,
The yellow wreckage of Lake Michigan—
The unpredictable first breath of a day
Where I grew up depended on the wind.

My life would turn tail like a weathervane
And find attention wrung out on the line,
My breath in dollops, dead frogs in the throat,
The drill in the forehead, branches of membrane
Flocking with soot, or the unhallowed dregs
Of the lake come lapping up like burlap dogs.

Led by the nose around the pit of self
In all directions, I was washerwoman,
The dying year-god, infidel at the gate,
The egg of the world, machine-man, rancid goat.
But if the wind was veering, backing off,
They choked themselves on metamorphosis.

O Lux, Mazola, Wolf Lake, Standard Oil,
O city dump, O docks of Bethlehem—
Though a mind, run through its middle, can't forget
What creatures reamed its baffling passages,
In the dead calm of morning once, I rose
Breathless without your help, and walked away.

The Famine of Reason

Though language glitters when we eat,
Like knives and forks, and all our wares—
Cut-flowers and gossip, gilded chairs,
The mannerly hoisting of our meat—
Confuse for a time our deeper wars;
Though posture stiffens our belief
That what surrounds us is ourselves,
And lip-stained gloves and napkins come
Between us and the taste of grief,
My dear, once turning face to face
Past these embellishments of grace,
We shall become our ancestors:
Like them, dependent for our lives
On the wet corners of our mouths,
On that frank matter in the eye
That utters *friend* or *enemy,*
Like two beasts meeting in a tree.

Song in the Dead of Summer

She has gone with the goats.
Moss-light afoot, they move
Gradually through the clefts
Down to the elm grove,

And the way of the hoof
Lies cloven by the moon;
Under the arching horn
It goes as deep as bone.

Deeper than bone or grain,
The path without a gate
Descends and disappears
Like water at the root,

Like time between the stars,
Like wind, the last goat
And the hill go under grass
Where the inhuman wait.

She has gone dark with goats
To the pit of the year,
And autumn, the scavenger,
Crouches behind the dawn.

Chrysalis

Tent caterpillars, nesting in fruit trees,
Are best removed with the affected branches,
The book said, and so I pruned them down.

And while I soaked their webs with kerosene,
I watched those thousands, ochre, blue, and black,
Writhing in pain where apples would have been.

My skin crawled with them into their gauzy tents
Where sunlight tightened, reddened like the day.
I wondered whether they would sing as they burned

And turn to something else. I lit a match
To touch them, and went up in smoke,
Cracked in the flame, fell down, and rolled away.

When the skin came off my face, I saw it roll
Away from the burns in layers, brittle and clear
As edges of egg-white turning from a fire.

And when my hand came out of its cocoon
In a fluttery sweat, beating itself to life
Against the light in a room where nurses stood

Piecing facts together, it rose to my face,
Burning as though still burning, in pink tatters.
It wrinkled skinny wings before my eyes.

It shook in the air, leafing itself sideways,
Hovered afraid an inch from my forehead,
Then sank against it gradually to rest.

The Satirists

With verminous ringlets leaping on their wigs,
They staggered through the city, stuttering rage
At a world pulled inside out by hypocrites.
Lace to their elbows, elbows steeped in swill,
The carpet-knights answered like Latin-mongers;
The acrobats and prigs guffawed in the dark
To praise, like cats, the tickling end of the quill.

Oh indignation lit their cheeks like chilblains,
And while their gouty great-toes pulsed on the stones,
Gin Lane flocked out to chorus, "Up smocks all!"
Ambition rolled with Simony in the streets
Where life lay squeezed into its opposites.
"Reform!" they shouted, but their voices wheezed
Like drainpipes through an ever-thickening phlegm.
"Blindmen!" they cried, and jumped out of their shoes,
But still the pock-faced pimps gnawed at the moon.

Toasting themselves in black and yellow bile,
They turned splenetic wisdom to the wall,
Weeping for Donkeys and the City of Christ
Or country pleasures beaten into holes.
Those great, blood-let, exacerbated men—
Foredoomed to choke like thieves on their own tongues—
All muttered, "Cover your hearts and trim them close,"
While they lurched home to cork anonymous wives.

Advice to the Orchestra

Start like pieces of string:
Lank homeliness attached, maybe, to nothing.
Then oh! my harpies, brush over the rows and thrust
Music like brooms under their chairs, rouse out the cats, the purses,
    and the dust.
Make them all leap up—the ophthalmic trance-breakers, the dog-
    gers, midge-killers, all the pie-faced gawkies and their
    crumbs.
Give them music to break their glasses, to knock their eyelids up like
    hatbrims.

When they run, follow them out of doors, out of windows,
Assault their tails with chorts and tootles, oompahs and glissandos.
Snare them. Give them no hiding places. Let them be draked in the
    reeds.
Slide after them into dumps and suburbs, over trembling hairpin
    roads,
Across channels and bays to the tilted islands where water whirls on
    edge.
Spiral through tunnels, over the baffling rocks and the spokes of
    forests, to the last desperate wheelprint, committing out-
    rage.

Oh my outlandish ones,
Offer yourselves through the mold on brass, through skins and
    bones.
Your music must consume its instruments
Or die lost in the elbow-joints and valves, in snaggle and crook,
    ratchet and pinchbeck, in the folded winds.
Let the boom come. Send up the burning brows,
The white domes of your echoes.

Stand in the pit. Strike the sides of your death. Let spherical thunder
Rise from gravel-throated, unharmonious earth, the stricken center,

Beyond air fringed like a curtain, through the cabbage leaves and
       angels of the moon,
The mercurial archangels,—rise to untune
The principalities and powers, the squash of the sun, virtues and
       jovial dominations, the saturnine thrones, calliope-pump-
       ing cherubim and seraphim with their heads ablaze
Against the old gods' mobile, eccentric knees.

The Starlings

We beat our pans with sticks,
Shook ratchets and hand-bells,
And watched the starlings rise
Into reluctant flocks
Whose noise grew mad as ours.
They circled a few blocks,
Then sank back into place
Around our cornices.
They listened, motionless,
To recorded cries of hawks
And starlings in distress.
A stream from a fire-hose,
Breaking and washing windows,
Gave them a good carouse.
Phosphorous cats on wires,
Stuffed owls, and roman candles
Were simply part of the night
To starlings used to stars
And all our other tricks.

Pigeons on statues
Of horse-backed conquerors
Show to be bird-stained
Is not a loss of face;
Sparrows, dropping behind
Horses, pave the way
For grand processionals;
But starlings ride only starlings
Up the façades of buildings
And won't give back a foot,
Spurring, fit to break
All spirits but their own
For roosts on the edge of nothing.

And if they fall, as some
Did when we shot them,
A starling in the hand—
Green breast and starry back—
Crouching wrongside-up,
Won't move for anyone.

The First Day of a Search

We hunted a boy lost on the frozen lake.
While sunlight flattened and turned blue,
Marshgrass in rattling tussocks nosed the ice
Like giant muskrats whickering in their fur.
Numb in the wind and slipshod, we crossed over
Inlets and narrows, skirted open flaws
Where water, heaving, slid beside and below
A thin crust perched, like weather, on its back.

Cautious and slow at first, we carried boards,
Ladders and carpets like our own islands
To the crackling edges and lay down on them
As though we'd come to sleep till the spring thaws;
But the cold rose up and tightened at our brows,
And when we walked again, parting at random,
Each held his life more carelessly in his hands,
Seeing the hard clouds blacken and spill forward.

Nothing for miles was taller than a boy.
This is the ice, we said, and there's the world.
To break through one is not to find the other.
He would have leaped aside, we said. But wept.
By snow like wave-crests in the reeds, we stopped
And, cupping our ears, heard only our own breath
Drifting from mouth to forehead where it curled
And closed above us like the shrivelling day.

All night, we called aloud. What answered was
Ice, or the darkness dreaming its own echoes,
Or landlocked water ageing below our feet.
One aimed a flashlight at the sky, and the flakes fell
To the cone's unwavering tip like a whirlpool.
Another fired a flare; it burst and shot

Petals and starfish down to dazzle us,
And we were white on both shores of our eyes.

Before an ugly dawn, one fell to his knees,
Clumsy with love and stupor, watching his light
Skid to the water and go splashing downward.
Staring through suddenly translucent ice,
He saw his own shape frozen under glass
With snails and ribbonweed in a solid garden
And, from his thrusting palms,—the light flashed out—
Saw cracks like lightning break across his face.

Out for a Night

It was No, no, no, practicing at a chair,
And No at the wall, and one for the fireplace,
And down the stairs it was No over the railing,
And two for the dirt, and three Noes for the air,

And four in a row rapidly over the bar,
Becoming Maybe, Maybe, from spittoon to mirror,
It was shrugging cheeks on one face after another,
And Perhaps and So-So at both ends of a cigar,

Five, and it was Yes as a matter of fact
Who said it wasn't all the way down the bottle,
It was Hell Yes over and lightly underfoot,
And tongue like a welcome mat for the bartender,

And Yes in the teeth, Yes like a cracked whistle,
And one for you, and two for the rest of us,
Indeed, Indeed, the chair got up on the table,
And Yes got up on the chair and kissed the light

And the light burned, and Yes fell out of the chair,
And the chair slid off the table, and it was Maybe
All over the floor, tilted, it was squat,
And plunge to the rear, and smack lips like a baby,

It was five for the fingers Absolutely,
Four in the corners, it was three for the show,
And two descending eyebrows to make a ceiling,
And No to the knees and chin, and one Goodbye.

On the Dosewallips Bridge

Broad daylight stretches from an oyster bed
Across a salt marsh to a whitened coast
Where geese, blown back as fast as they can fly,
Hover a moment, yaw, then slope away.
With rivets creaking, girders overhead
Take on the live weight of the wind and sigh.
I lean against the railing and hang on.

Below my feet a current, fast enough
To swivel cutthroat trout before the tide,
Goes blue in riffles, clear to its bedrock.
Men from this railing fish or shoot at geese
Or give themselves more weight than they can bear
And knock along the riverbed like stones.
A river goes one way. Whatever goes

Over the railing heavier than wind
Will take the channel as a matter of course
And come to nothing, windward, in the sea.
With scale and stick, an engineer could trace
The insignificant resultant force
My body makes on the most distant strut,
All the component stresses, pound by pound,

Throughout the trussed-up framework, calculate
The strain on I-beams if I stamp my foot,
How much I mean to the last nut and bolt
In flexion, torsion, as a jam or shear,
My imposition on the riverside,
On stanchions, pilings buried out of sight
In shale where the old streamers put their bones.

Now air and water, the whole raft of weather
Hogging and sinking, rippling out of phase,

Blown high to snow or rivering to salt
But blanking into whiteness either way,
Collide with me. I turn, and the wind blows.
Relieved of my dead weight, the bridge might sway
A fraction less from the true. I walk across.

Writing to Order

Standing on the floor,
I join some furniture
In front of a window—
A table and a chair.
Other men elsewhere
Are plugging what they know
By doing something next,
Stretching in sequence
Across their separate days
Like laces through eyelets.

I see them steering cars
Or bunching on corners,
The good buyers and sellers
Held up by the lights,
Who all know what to do
With blanks and fountain pens:
They scribble through the bars,
They follow suits indoors,
Impressing customers
Like carbons through tablets.

Glad-handed, there they go
Up stairs in breathless flights
On elevator shoes
Against a shaft of air
Into the highest flats
Where goods, like services
Laid on an altar, grow—
At a great sacrifice—
Abundant for all those
Writing to order.

Here, beside furniture
Which even death-cells use

To prop a prisoner—
A table and a chair—
I face what I don't know,
Can't follow or wait for,
The private enterprise
For which there's no demand,
The shoe on the wrong foot,
No laces to pull tight.

My left hand in a sweat
Is shaking in my right.
Here on this tabletop,
No one can co-sign.
No flimsy order-blank
X'd on the dotted line
Can show me how to write
Over my signature
Looped like a bow-knot
A consequential truth.

That Old Gang of Mine

"Warden, I thank you." "Not at all." He bowed.
With my dress cane, I hit him on the head.

"A stirring evening, Officer." The guard
Blinked at my spinning watch-chain. Then he snored.

"Come out, good thieves," I whispered to the walls,
And heard the fine teeth mousing in the cells.

Sliding the key-ring under the cold bars,
I tiptoed down the hall and out of doors.

The first explosion coughed the windows out;
The second made stones generous to a fault;

The third threw up the prison, clapped its wings,
Squinted the lights, and pierced the sirens' lungs.

Over the rubble in their shredded suits,
Out of the tangle of bent license plates,

Through the dim ruckus between dust and guns,
Came my key men, the unlocked skeletons,

Bumping their knobby knees against the rocks
That once stood tall as hell to shepherd crooks.

"Run for our lives!" I whispered. "First comes grass,
Then shrubs, then trees, then water, and then grace."

Oscar the Bounder ripped his jacket off
And vaulted toward the deep night in the buff.

Phineas the Mouthpiece staggered, his eyes shut,
And hawked to break the thick years in his throat.

Sylvester the One-man Sack-race, self-possessed,
Stalked through the brambles, lofty as a post.

Esau the Actor, two feet, four feet, none,
Rose past the willows, flickered, and was gone.

Then out of the heap, the unpacked bloodhounds came
Groggy but eager, snuffling the old game.

Fit to be tied behind them, stumbling guards
Saw their long leashes snarling into braids

As we went crosspath, taking to our heels
In five directions, tireless through the hills.

At dawn, across the water, over the dunes,
Past the bleak alders and the bleaker downs,

Over the thorn scrub like *cheval-de-frise,*
I went to meet them, purple with their praise,

And as we leaped and crowed in a shower of cash,
We danced a ring around the burning bush.

The Carcass

Wading upstream under the cedar boughs,
I found a headless dead one in the rain.
It lay on moss, as large as a crumpled man.

It had no fur, no skin. There were no flies
On the bare stretch of its back, no stain
On the bank, no dying in water or air.

The heart or the gizzard gleamed, liver or lights,
And the wet flanks—or was the breast the groin?
I could make neither head nor tail of it. Then,

I saw the sprawling, two-foot, spatulate flippers,
Leathery from the trunk. Three miles from a river,
Twenty miles from the sea, there are no monsters,

Not for a man awake. But here was one.
It was no commonplace or circus creature,
No heap of matter, stuff or pet of the brain.

It had come all the lumbering way ashore
Through rapids and drifts, past wharf rats and tributaries,
Steeping the falls, slewfooted as a walrus,

Half up a mountain where the creeks turn thin,
Dipping in silted grottoes and green elbows,
To meet its master—had that been a man?—

And be flayed to the quick. My feet sank in my boots.
Someone had driven it to earth. So few
Exist, their deaths alone are trophies.

It was so freshly washed, so clean of its coat,
I looked around for the knife-edge of the hero,
Wiping his profile on the bedded moss.

I looked for nothing, then slapped my palm on the water.
A hawk burst from the tallest visible pine.
The flippers were two tails of enormous beavers

That had been ringed like tree-trunks and peeled bare
Of their hides over their muddy shoulders
And left as one under the pelting rain.

A Day in the City

Dismounting from stools and benches, pouring through bars,
Let's do the day up brown,
Knock it back like a short drink, get off our trolley,
Put our foot downtown.

There, cutting the sun in half with our eyelids,
Sinister with love,
We shall wait till those feet, swollen to thousands on the pavement,
Are aching to move.

Then from the joints at our knees, the crooks at our elbows,
From all the hugging sides,
Through the calves and hams, the perpendicular marches
Will drill us into squads.

Rising from cornerstones, cripples with bristling pencils
Will jam on their caps
And join us—the floorwalkers and shoplifters, gulls and barkers,
The blindmen in their cups,

And the chirruping children, the sailors and loaded Indians,
Fur-bearing stylish stouts,
All thronging from broken curb to curb and up the lamp-posts,
Onto ledges like goats.

And the city is ours. See, the bridges all give up, the arcades
Rattle their silver shops,
Buildings chip in, the sidewalks roll over like dogs, hotels
Chime their fire-escapes.

Here on a glittering carpet of plate glass go dancing
Till leggings and bandages
Trail us like trains round the fountain to the plaza, till our faces
Leap from our jaws,

And our sleeves roll back to the trombones and armbands,
And, shooting the mailchutes,
We stand in circles on every floor, shaking our palms,
Flagging our bedsheets.

We shall trump up a total noise, a silence battered
Like rams in the air.
Let the sewers hoot, all risers drop their treads
To the wrenched foot of the stair.

Then quietly, left and right, with our bandoliers
Crossed on our blouses,
We shall drift away through the empty business-ends of the streets
To go back to pieces,

While the city lets out the fiery-red, grumbling water-wagons
To lay the dust,
And sends toward our houses, through every alley,
The huge, defaced,

Skulking, familiar, handle-breaking, off-key garbageman
Who had been killed,
But who now heaps under the raised lids, our old lives
Before they are cold.

Standing Halfway Home

At the last turn in the path, where locust thorns
Halter my sleeve, I suddenly stand still
For no good reason, planting both my shoes.
No other takes its place when my noise ends.
The hush is on. Through the deserted boughs,
Through fireweed, bracken, duff, down to the ground,
The air comes as itself without a sound
And deepens at my knees like waste of breath.

Behind my back lies the end of property;
Ahead, around a corner, a new house.
Barbed wire and aerials cross up and out
To mark the thresholds of man's common sense:
Keep out, keep talking. Doing neither one,
Here, central and inert, I stop my mouth
To reassure all the invisible
For whom my sight and sound were dangerous.

Eyes in the wings of butterflies stare through
The hazel leaves. Frozen beside my foot,
A tawny skink relaxes on its toes.
I shift my weight. The sun bears down the hill,
And overhead, past where an eye can turn,
A hiss of feathers parts the silence now.
At my arm's length a seedy, burr-sized wren,
As if I were a stalk, bursts into song.

On Seeing an X-Ray of My Head

Now face to face, hard head, old nodder and shaker,
While we still have ears,
Accept my congratulations: you survived
My headlong blunders
As, night by night, my knuckles beat at your brow
More often than at doors,
Yet you were pampered, waved from the end of your stick
Like a bird in feathers,
Wrapped in towels, whistled and night-capped,
And pressed into pillows.
I see by this, the outline of our concern,
What you will lose
Before too long: the shadowy half of chin
And prodding nose,
Thatchwork of hair, loose tongue, and parting lips,
My look as blank as yours,
And yet, my madcap, catch-all rattlepot,
Nothing but haze
Shows on this picture what we had in mind,
The crannied cauliflower
Ready to boil away at a moment's notice
In a fit of vapors
And leave us holding the bag. Oh my brainpan,
When we start our separate ways
With opaque, immortal fillings clenched in our teeth
Like a bunch of keys,
And when your dome goes rolling into a ditch
And, slack in the jaws,
Stops at a hazard, some unplayable lie,
Accept at your ease
Directly what was yours at one remove:
Light through your eyes,
Air, dust, and water as themselves at last. Keep smiling.
Consider the source.
Go back to the start, old lime-pit, remembering flesh and skin,
Your bloody forebears.

Every Good Boy Does Fine

I practiced my cornet in a cold garage
Where I could blast it till the oil in drums
Boomed back; tossed free-throws till I couldn't move my thumbs;
Sprinted through tires, tackling a headless dummy.

In my first contest, playing a wobbly solo,
I blew up in the coda, alone on stage,
And twisting like my hand-tied necktie, saw the judge
Letting my silence dwindle down his scale.

At my first basketball game, gangling away from home
A hundred miles by bus to a dressing room,
Under the showering voice of the coach, I stood in a towel,
Having forgotten shoes, socks, uniform.

In my first football game, the first play under the lights
I intercepted a pass. For seventy yards, I ran
Through music and squeals, surging, lifting my cleats,
Only to be brought down by the safety man.

I took my second chances with less care, but in dreams
I saw the bald judge slumped in the front row,
The coach and team at the doorway, the safety man
Galloping loud at my heels. They watch me now.

You who have always horned your way through passages,
Sat safe on the bench while some came naked to court,
Slipped out of arms to win in the long run,
Consider this poem a failure, sprawling flat on a page.

Filling Out a Blank

High School Profile-Achievement Form for D. Wagoner, 1943
... Item 8, Job Preferences: 1) *Chemist* 2) *Stage Magician* 3)——

My preference was to be
The shrewd man holding up
A test-tube to the light,
Or the bowing charlatan
Whose inexhaustible hat
Could fill a stage with birds.
Lying beyond that,
Nothing seemed like me.

Imagining the years
In a smock or a frock coat
Where all was black or white,
Idly I set about
To conjure up a man
In a glare, concocting life
Like a rich precipitate
By acid out of base.

What shivered up my sleeve
Was neither rabbit nor gold,
But a whole bag of tricks:
The bubbling of retorts
In sterile corridors,
Explosions and handcuffs,
Time falling through trapdoors
In a great cloud of smoke.

But the third guess leaves me cold:
It made me draw a blank,
A stroke drawn with my pen
Going from left to right
And fading out of ink
As casually as a fact.
It came to this brief line,
This disappearing act.

The Observer

The woman kneeling by the side of the road
Sketches a porcupine lying dead,
Its tail on pavement, chest on the narrow shoulder.
The waxed face of the moon wears through the sky.
She turns a page and reaches out to touch
The quills left upright on the scruff of its neck.
Rising, she circles, and a car sweeps by:
The trailing wind goes past her, and the dust
Swerves to a standstill, hovers, and falls down.

For an hour, I've waited while the night sank in,
And now she takes her loose windbreaker sleeve
To drag the spiny heap over the gravel
And into the weeds, breaking a foxglove
Against its side as if by accident.

I join her to see the black soles of its paws,
Yellow incisors grinning in profile,
Its pale-tipped jaggers aimed from the dead center.
Thrusting dim lights ahead, another car
Drags its pursuing vacuum down the line.
We hold ourselves against the buffeting,
Then walk toward our house and a level bed;
But on the bank she trips out of one sandal
And, sitting down without it, holds her head.

She knows a porcupine is drawn from its life
Or—like the quills shoved out the other side
Of flesh because the irreversible barbs
Take one way out—takes this way out of death.
I rub her foot. No need to mention love.